UNSCRIPTED

Experiences of a Hospice Volunteer,
the Joy in the Journey, and
Thoughts on End of Life Care

LESLEY ANDRUS

BALBOA.
PRESS

A DIVISION OF HAY HOUSE

Balboa Press books may be ordered through booksellers or by contacting:

Balboa Press
A Division of Hay House
1663 Liberty Drive
Bloomington, IN 47403
www.balboapress.com
1 (877) 407-4847

Because of the dynamic nature of the Internet, any web addresses or links contained in this book may have changed since publication and may no longer be valid. The views expressed in this work are solely those of the author and do not necessarily reflect the views of the publisher, and the publisher hereby disclaims any responsibility for them.

The author of this book does not dispense medical advice or prescribe the use of any technique as a form of treatment for physical, emotional, or medical problems without the advice of a physician, either directly or indirectly. The intent of the author is only to offer information of a general nature to help you in your quest for emotional and spiritual well-being. In the event you use any of the information in this book for yourself, which is your constitutional right, the author and the publisher assume no responsibility for your actions.

Any people depicted in stock imagery provided by Thinkstock are models, and such images are being used for illustrative purposes only. Certain stock imagery © Thinkstock.

Printed in the United States of America.

ISBN: 978-1-4525-2237-1 (sc)
ISBN: 978-1-4525-2239-5 (hc)
ISBN: 978-1-4525-2238-8 (e)

Library of Congress Control Number: 2014916676

Balboa Press rev. date: 10/16/2014

To Paula Caputo –
   whose persistence, encouragement, editorial support and true
   friendship brought this book into being

   -- and special thanks to my friends
   Terry, Page, Lyn, Rebekah, Ruth, Ellen and Joyce

CONTENTS

PREFACE

I had never heard of Hospice until the week before my husband died. It was late. The help they could offer was minimal. He died the day the movers arrived to pack our things. It had been his dream – to change our lives, to build a house and move out of the city into a small, beautiful mountain town where we had vacationed.

The town had always been a happy place for us. We fished, played golf, rode bikes, hiked and in the winter we skied. It was our special family place – minimal interruptions from the outside world. It was a place of fun and happy memories.

So I was not surprised that he chose to leave us on the eve of a new life. He had been very sick, the cancer eating through his entire body. My young sons and I watched helplessly. Through the months of his pain and slow deterioration, 850 miles away we were building a new house, a place for a new beginning. Gently and quietly, the eve before our departure he left us to start our new life in a place that held only memories of happiness.

Since then I have learned much about death and dying as I became a Hospice volunteer in my new hometown. As I have assisted patients, participating in the final days and hours, sometimes helping, sometimes watching helplessly in their final journey, I have learned about living. I hope the sharing of my experiences and observations may resonate in some small way and may provide a new lens through which to view life, and help caregivers and patients learn in the final days how to live the ending without fear and with dignity and love.

THE RIGHTS OF A HOSPICE PATIENT

In my Hospice training I was given a sheet of paper listing the rights of our patients. I reviewed it. The rights sounded logical if not self-evident. I put it away. Recently, in thinking about how to organize my stories, I came across the list and realized that many of my experiences and observations were about patients trying to assert these rights, while families sometimes acknowledged them and other times seemed to be unaware.

The burdens of caring for a dying family member can be exhausting. With resources, both financial and emotional, being daily challenged, it is often difficult to pull back and view life from the patient's point of view. Sometimes we feel we know what is best and charge ahead. There may be good and rational reasons for our conduct, but sometimes our efficiency is distressing to our patient, and may even be counter- productive to our goal of easing their pain.

Recently I noticed that the chair beside my patient's bed had been switched from a comfortable arm chair to a utilitarian commode – a metal chair with a small cushion covering a portable toilet. My patient was upset. The chair was not only uncomfortable for her visitors, but it was in her direct line of sight, a constant reminder of her increasing frailty and a transformation, albeit small, of her bedroom sanctuary into a hospital room. She asked her caregiver to remove it. Her family brought it back. Perhaps had they been able to understand how the sight of that chair affected her, an alternative placement – satisfying their concerns and her sensibilities – could have been achieved.

In reviewing the stories I wrote over the years about my observations and experience with Hospice patients, I realized that the issues raised in the list of patient rights formed the basis of most of the stories. Many patient issues overlap. Many can be addressed and some cannot. With an understanding and acknowledgement of the concerns articulated in the patient's bill of rights, the last days of life can be better for all.

THE RIGHT TO BE IN CONTROL

Grant me the right to make as many decisions as possible regarding my care. Please do not take choices from me. Let me make my own decisions.

As the body becomes frail and mental acuity dims, many decisions about a patient's care are by necessity taken over and dictated by the caregiver, leaving the patient with little control over his or her life. To the extent that we can allow our patient to make decisions, to be given choices, it provides a sense of control over life. Sometimes there is no possibility of control, such as giving a patient drugs for self-administering when that patient has lost all sense of time. However, even in these situations, acknowledgement of the loss may give comfort and encourage focus on other areas where the patient may still have some measure of input.

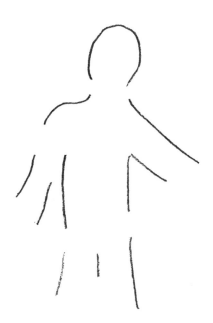

DISAPPEARING

As he struggled to climb out of the car, he looked up at me and said, "I'm disappearing."

It's true that his diminutive body no longer stood tall, strong. He no longer ran marathons, trekked the Himalayas, biked over summits. Now he was hunched over, shoulders rounded, head forward, gaze downward willing his legs to move, first one foot, then the other, slowly, an inch at a time. His body was physically shrinking, curling up into itself. He was 82 and had Parkinson's disease.

"You know how you come to an open door and you just walk right through it," he said to me as we approached his front door. "Well, did you know that Parkinson's patients can't do that. I stand here but my legs freeze. They just don't want to move forward, to go through." His legs eventually moved and we went through the door, but I could see the extreme concentration and of course it took more time.

Everything now takes more time. Getting dressed becomes more of an ordeal. Things he did easily his whole life, like putting his arm through a sleeve, no longer is a rote movement. His arm goes into a space, but it's hard to find that space. He puts his hand through the wrong hole and gets tangled. Things he did since he was a kid, with no thought, automatic, now are overwhelmingly difficult. He no longer wears shoes with laces.

He wants to be able to do simple things for himself, but now everyone is waiting and watching while he tries to put his zipper together and pull it up. Even when his hands don't shake, he has difficulty finding that little groove for the zipper end. I watch. Seeing his struggle, I offer to help but I know he wants to be able to do this little thing so he declines my offer. He is aware I am waiting and watching, which of course makes him more nervous. Now his hands do shake. He can't get it. Three seconds feel like three minutes – for both of us. He is cognizant that I am waiting. He doesn't want to now ask for help, but I am certain he is uncomfortable being the center of attention and perhaps worrying that my patience is waning. He doesn't want to go through this every time he goes out so it's easier to stay home, to sit, to not move, to not get dressed.

I know all these thoughts are going through his brain. I don't want to make him uncomfortable. I am okay with waiting, but if I tell him, I know that may make him even more nervous. Should I reach over and pull up that zipper, or should I turn away and create a diversion for myself, releasing him from the spotlight?

It is not just the physical difficulty of dressing or walking. I see the confusion and slowness permeating his brain. "I have a hard time in group conversations," he told me. He was intelligent, kept himself apprised of world events, and always had an opinion. "The problem is," he explained, "by the time I formulate what I want to say on the topic being discussed, everyone has moved on to another subject. They're finished with my topic." Even his voice is getting softer so that I often must ask him to repeat what he said. All of these things make him feel increasingly excluded from conversation. He is physically disappearing.

In a moment of introspection, he said to me, "I am like a wave in the ocean. I started big, curling and crashing forward, moving everything in front of me. But now I have crested, I am losing speed, thinning out, slowing down. I am sinking into the sand. I am disappearing."

I could sense the sadness, the feeling of loss, like the powerful ocean wave that dissipates slowly until not even a faint trace of its outline exists. What was once there, so significant in size and strength, is now gone. But there is also a peace in that image, a completion, a return full circle to the warmth of the earth. It is just hard to feel the rightness of it when all you see is you, disappearing.

DRIVING

He was a young 48 when the brain tumor took control of his life. He was sleeping when I arrived, a state that had been increasing with the growth of his tumor. His wife told me that he continued to indulge in one activity, a habit that most people realized was detrimental to one's health and should therefore be stopped. However, at this stage of his life, what was left of it, those concerns ceased to bother him. It was something to do, a form of entertainment, perhaps shaking a fist against fate. "When he wakes up, he will probably go into the garage for a smoke," his wife informed me.

I had been visiting him for several weeks. During that time he had been constantly falling, but now a change in medication had steadied his balance. It had also softened his tongue. Previously anger and accusations had spewed from his mouth. He constantly attacked his wife, her care, her being. While she knew it was the disease talking, it still hurt. It still felt like a dagger intentionally plunged into her exhausted, unappreciated body.

This day his wife and their 16 year old daughter -- talented, athletic and the epitome of grace and youth -- were going for a girls' lunch out, a chance to immerse in a few hours of normalcy. They would be close if I needed help, though a call, and indeed even the possibility of receiving such a call, created a reality from which their consciousness could never escape. I chose not to write down her cell phone number, hoping to give them this small space of time, though later wondering if the inability to communicate would only exacerbate their apprehension. Next time I will ask.

A short while after they left he woke. We talked about the television program that had played through his hours of sleep and wakefulness. We talked about his animals, the playful rambunctious shelter dog that seemed oblivious to the unfolding family trauma, and the independent cat that kept him company from a bed perched on his dresser. His speech was soft and sometimes slurred, requiring me to often repeat his words, or let them go lest repetition create frustration. A little balancing act.

He decided to get out of bed and informed me that it was time to take his pills. Medication – the bane of the terminally ill. The pain pills cause constipation, requiring another pill to relieve this problem. Each drug seemed to cause some unwanted, uncomfortable or painful effect so that each new pill administered for its beneficial effects required another pill to lessen or reverse its negative ones. His pills were in a divided plastic container, no longer marked for the days of the week, but rather the hours in the day – morning, noon, afternoon, evening and night. Days were now regimented. He found the appropriate ones and was able to swallow them without difficulty. Duty done he was now ready for his smoke.

Stepping into slippers next to the garage door, he maneuvered his way down the single step, grabbing on to the adjacent furnace for balance. The cigarettes and lighter were kept close in his pocket and easily retrieved and lit. There was a chair in the corner of the garage next to a small table containing a plastic glass with water – his safe ashtray. He paced around until he finished his cigarette, and then walked through the garage door into the snow, heading straight for his car. "I need to start it up, to make sure the engine is still running," he told me. I tried to assure him that his daughter undoubtedly used it recently and was therefore confident that the battery was not dead. He ignored my assertions and began looking for the keys. They were not in the ignition, under the seat or in the center console. He moved haltingly around the car to the passenger side, opening that door and searching the glove compartment. No keys. I sighed with relief, though still contemplating my conduct (jump in the passenger seat, try to turn off the ignition, pull on the emergency hand break if there were one) in the event he was able to start the car. After another walk around the car, he realized the keys were not there – "Probably in my daughter's room upstairs," he speculated, showing no signs of retrieving them. I relaxed.

As he finished his second cigarette, dousing it in his plastic cup and emptying the cup, water and all, into the garbage can, his wife and daughter drove up. "He was hoping to find the keys to start up the car and ensure it was running," I explained. This was obviously a frequent occurrence as his wife told me that is why they had hidden the keys. As they walked past him his daughter said in a flat, matter of fact tone of voice, "You cannot drive any more, Dad."

Her 48 year old father -- no longer competent to function outside the house, now requiring constant supervision, a shuffling, aging man, unable to shave and losing the facility for dressing. Car keys – the symbol of freedom and movement. Gone. What did he feel when he heard the words, "You cannot drive any more, Dad."

THE RIGHT TO HAVE A SENSE OF PURPOSE

I have lost my job. I can no longer fulfill my role in my family. Please help me find some new sense of purpose.

At this point in life the patient is losing his or her identity. She may have been an executive in a big company, or he may have run a family business, but now neither goes to an office. No one seeks their advice. No one acknowledges their ability or authority. Even in the family setting, the patient may no longer be a provider or caregiver. How to give a sense of purpose in such a circumstance?

Clearly the traditional concept of purpose is no longer applicable as the patient may no longer be able to "do" or "provide." But purpose comes not just from doing. It also comes from feeling needed and valued.

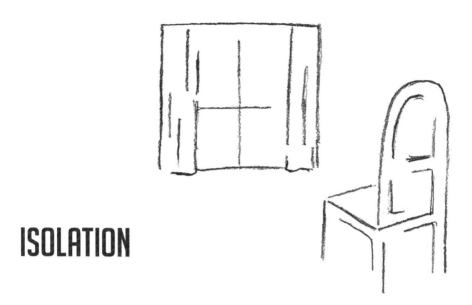

ISOLATION

My patient had gone through a difficult time period in her life, experiencing extreme depression and attempting suicide. She had survived, moved to this small mountain town and started a new life. Now however with Parkinson's consuming her body, she was again having moments of depression.

"How do you deal with this sadness?" I ask.

"I try to live one moment at a time," she explains. "I get up in the morning and ask myself, "Do I shower this morning, or is it my day to swim? I go through my closet and pick out something colorful, something I haven't worn in a while to make me feel different from yesterday. I may remember something I heard on the news last night and decide to write my congressman, though I do need help for that as I can't see well and sometimes my shaky hand makes writing a little too difficult and impossible to read."

"Do you know why you feel sad?" I ask.

"Because I am alone. I am not really connected any more. I don't go out to the symphony, to the theatre, to dinner," her voice echoing in loss. She is tethered to an oxygen machine and while her caregiver does have a portable tank, it is an effort and now just used for those necessities, like doctor's appointments and therapy, or a few little personal things to make her feel better, like a haircut or manicure. There is so much less of a connection to the outside world.

"Also, everything I was is now gone," she explains. "Everything that defined me, or that I allowed myself to be defined by – I was a dancer, a mother, a producer, an assistant to an oceanographer, a wife, a lover. I am no longer these things. I am peripheral."

But it is not only the loss of identity that she feels now. In her mind there is something worse -- "I have nothing to offer," she says. "I am just here, waiting for people to come to me, for something to happen to me."

How do I tell her how untrue is her last statement? How can I even describe what she has given to me? Two days a week for over two years she has shared her life, her hopes, her dreams, her regrets. We have lively debates about the state of the world, religion, prejudice, technology, the environment, immigration, health, children, friends. She has stimulated my brain, made me think, and now she is my editor, helping me share all these stories.

She still has her interest in the world, her imagination and her sense of humor. It is hard to focus on these things when her physical life, like her vision, continues to dim, and daily she becomes less connected to everything around her. How can we give our patients a sense of purpose in light of these physical failings?

Then I realized that

- by listening to the stories of her life, I am validating her existence
- by bringing in articles to discuss and debate, I am acknowledging the importance of her opinion

- by writing about her thoughts and feelings, I am allowing her to leave written evidence of her life
- by soliciting her opinion and editorial comments on my stories, I am giving her an opportunity to contribute
- by simply listening I am telling her how important she is to me, how much needed.

All of these activities give her a purpose, something to look forward to, a validation of her worth, her being, her life. I tell her.

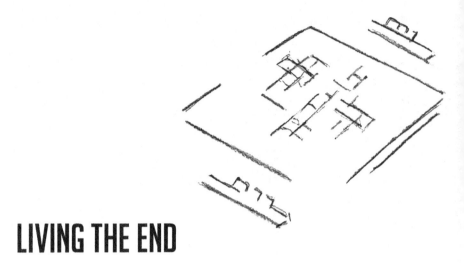

LIVING THE END

One of the things I absolutely love about Hospice work is that I never know what new experience I am going to have. In some respects it reminds me of my old profession as a trial lawyer and the old maxim that there are three arguments – the one you prepare, the one you actually give, and the one you think of as soon as you walk out of the courtroom.

With Hospice patients you are given background on their condition and situation, and what you are expected to do. You then arrive and may find that the patient desires or needs something completely different. Of course, after you leave you think of things you could have done.

I knew my new patient was on heavy oxygen, fairly immobile but conscious. I was simply to stay with her to allow her husband a break to go cross country skiing. When I entered their apartment, I found a very alert woman. She was not in bed, but sitting up, fully dressed and ready for company. Easy conversation ensued until finally the patient reminded her husband that he needed to leave if he wanted to ski and to take advantage of my presence. He left.

She had led an active life – home, family, and a full time job. In her retirement she started drawing cartoons. She had assembled quite a book. They were about retirement and her husband's changing expectations – after all, from his perspective she was now free and available to cook gourmet meals, plan special outings and attend to his every comfort. The cartoons were funny, wonderfully sketched and focused so poignantly on those universal differences between man and woman. Now she had become tethered to her oxygen canister, and in the face of a closing of life she was pouring her energies into her creations.

After sharing her art with me, I asked if there was anything I could do for her. "Why yes," she responded. "I need a haircut. I always did it myself but this time I messed it up. It needs some correcting," she said.

Haircut! I couldn't believe it. That certainly hadn't been in my job description. I had trimmed my sons' hair when they were young, but somehow that seemed quite different. Sure – why not? I was a little intimidated when she directed me to a drawer that contained professional sheers and combs and other such items that would be found in a hair salon. I selected a scissors and comb and started trimming. When I finished she felt the back of her neck and announced it was perfect, but then there were no mirrors around and I didn't offer one. She felt good now. Her appearance was still important.

"Now, how about a game of scrabble?" she asked. We played three or four games and she trounced me every time. I was hoping for a comeback and chance to give her another challenge, but she died a short time later. Until the end she remained confined to her apartment, alert, well dressed and coiffed, living each day and looking toward tomorrow, an opportunity for another cartoon, and another game of scrabble.

BEAUTY

I found the trailer of my new Hospice patient. I parked and knocked on the door. A beautiful, petite woman met me. Petite is not really accurate – she was waiflike. When I subsequently got to know her and put my arms around her, I felt her fragility. I was afraid to give her a real hug for fear of breaking her thin frame. Oh, but the face! She had magnificent skin. It was hard to believe she was in her late sixties. And there she was beautifully made up – eye makeup, lipstick and a pretty wig, though it was obvious she couldn't see the back as it was matted and slightly askew. I thought about suggesting I comb out the back, but I refrained. She was obviously one who took great care about her appearance and I did not want to make her feel as if she were deficient in the narrowing part of her life over which she had control.

Every Monday I drove her to a town 90 miles away, for radiation treatment. Occasionally we stopped to do errands – she wanted to pick out cards to send to her friends or buy some other little items for which she had collected coupons. It was always a pleasant drive. And during those hours she told me about her life.

She had had a good husband. For most of her life they had a farm. They raised two sons and had worked hard. They also had a daughter, and that was the reason she had moved to our valley – to be close to her daughter in her last days. She had breast cancer.

Before moving here she sold a little bed and breakfast inn that she and her husband had operated before he died. Although I never saw pictures, I could imagine it – tidy, cute, little knickknacks and doilies and crocheted afghans over the chairs.

After her course of treatment was completed I did not see her for some time, though I knew our nurses were continuing to care for her. She then came back into my life in a very unusual way.

Standing in the lobby of a hotel before commencement of the state Hospice conference, I was talking with our director when one of our nurses came up and announced that our patient wanted to know if we could help her find a job. She had done housework and was looking for a placement to earn some money. The nurse chuckled, saying "I know we at Hospice take very good care of our patients, but I didn't know our talents extended to finding employment for them too."

"I'll hire her," I said. "I could use someone to help me a few hours a week and I can be very flexible."

So she started coming to my house once a week. So conscientious, so fragile. She always arrived dressed in pressed jeans and beautifully made up, with her wig still slightly askew in the back. I kept encouraging her to take breaks, to rest, to have something to eat. She never did. At Christmas she gave me a candle and a beautiful thank you note, but it was I who was grateful, who was thankful for her.

A few months before her death she went on a cruise with her family. Later her daughter showed me the pictures. My former patient and helper was beaming and beautiful. Before she left I knew this would be her last vacation and that she had little time. I knew that she would not be back to my house. She did call, so very concerned, and I sensed upset, that she was somehow letting me down. I assured her I would be okay and that I just wanted her to relax and enjoy her trip.

Near the end I went to see her but she was no longer conscious. The wig no longer graced her head. I was struck by her hair – it was lusciously full and a beautiful color. I wondered why she had worn her wig to the end. Maybe it was easier – one less struggle in a life that was a daily battle. I stroked her hand and said goodbye. Her positive attitude and the care she took of her physical appearance had created purpose in her life and given us beauty.

THE RIGHT TO REMINISCE

There has been pleasure in my life, moments of pride, moments of love. Please give me some time to recollect those moments. And please listen to my recollections.

The present may be fading but life holds many memories, and we remember the happy ones -- the moments of love, of pride, of pleasure. Many of us do not really know much about the younger days or earlier histories of our parents or relatives or friends. We have been involved in our own lives and have not had the time to listen. Now as they are at the end of their lives we can learn about the challenges they met, how they survived, what made them who they are, and what wisdom they acquired. Everyone has a need to be heard and understood. We can not only learn from our patients, parents and friends, but by simply listening we can give their lives validity.

MEMORIES

He was pulling his suspender over his shoulder as he walked down the hall toward me. Although in his mid-80's with cancer, he looked surprisingly healthy. He had a round full face, a head of white hair, slightly thinning, and a sturdy, former football player type body, a few extra pounds, but definitely not overweight. He smiled as I introduced myself.

We walked into the living room and sat down. Even though I had been briefed by Hospice, he was quick to tell me about his wife whom he had lost a year and a half ago – one week short of their 60th anniversary. "Tell me about her," I said. "How did you meet her?"

He was a teenager, working in a dry goods store. His boss apparently liked him for he suggested a date with his sister. However, the protective brother warned, "I want no funny business with her." Guess that was Texas short hand for treat her like a lady. So on the first date he took her to the "picture show" and dinner. Mindful of the admonition, as they stood on her front porch he shook her hand and said good night. Later through a friend he heard her summary of the date –"he was awfully shy, he didn't even kiss me goodnight." So on the next date he fixed that. For a reason unexplained, that was his last date with her.

One summer day in June two years later, he and a friend had decided to spend the weekend hunting. Since the county to which they were going was "dry," they stocked up on beer to insure a good time. As they were coasting through the neighboring town, he saw her. He put his arm out the window, waved and yelled hello. She waved back. "I know her," he told his friend. "I don't believe you," the friend said. Then the sirens started. Behind them a police car signaled them to pull over. He didn't say but the beer cans must have been in plain sight for the next thing he knew, the deputy pulled them out of the car, handcuffed them and took them to jail. Neither had money for bail, so they sat.

Later in the afternoon, in comes that beautiful girl, the one to whom he had waved. It turns out she saw the whole arrest and called her uncle -- the sheriff. He's not sure how she did it, but she got him out of jail. So during the next few weeks he drove over to that little town and courted her. They got married the first week of August – less than two months later.

They had had their arguments over the 60 years, he was quick to offer, but it was a good marriage. He talked about the home she made, the children they raised. Their family had moved from Texas to northern California, living in different small communities, and then finally back to Texas. He worked in construction and in ship yards. He was good with his hands. He could fix anything. His reminiscences were happy. He had had a good life. He missed his wife, his best friend.

As I drove away I realized the gifts we had just given each other. By letting him wander through and share his memories, his happy times, he let me see the life of a good and caring man - not famous, not rich, but full, happy and filled with love.

ETHICAL WILL

She was in her 80's and had three grown daughters. I had just attended a Hospice meeting where I learned about the ethical will – leaving not what you have earned but what you have learned. I told her about it. The idea is to tell your children about you, about your life, your dreams, your regrets, your hopes.

So many of us know so little about our parents. We know where they were born, where they lived, what career they chose, how many children they had, where they traveled – the factual details, the structure of their lives. We may know some of the hardships they faced, but we don't know the details – what they did to overcome those hardships, who if anyone helped them, what they learned, how it changed them, or most importantly, how they felt during those times. We know about some of their successes and career achievements, but we don't know what they sacrificed for those accomplishments and whether they had any regrets.

I suggested that we write a letter to each of her daughters. We started with the memory of the moment each daughter arrived, her feelings and fears. We progressed through each's childhood – funny incidents, scary accidents and happy reminiscences. Then we wrote about the elephant in the room - the major event that had never been discussed, that is the termination of her marriage, the mental devastation and the recovery. She acknowledged the help each daughter gave her. She asked for forgiveness. She expressed her hopes, dreams and wishes for each. She told them of her love.

It took us several months to complete these letters. We sat in her garden, surrounded by flowers. With ice tea on the table, an umbrella shading us from the warm sun, she talked and I took notes. I went home, typed up the notes, and brought them back. We would then revise, two or three times, with more memories and more thoughts. It was a project of love and openness and total honesty. It was fun. We laughed at some of her crazy reminiscences. It was heart wrenching, reliving her pain and struggles. It was emotionally satisfying, letting in the light and creating the precious gift of herself to her daughters.

THE RIGHT TO KNOW THE TRUTH AND TO BE IN DENIAL OF THE TRUTH

When you withhold the truth from me, you treat me as if I am no longer living. I am still living, and I need to know the truth about my life. Please help me find that truth. And if I hear the truth and choose not to accept it, that is my right.

Unless there is some mental impairment, patients should be part of the discussion concerning their health care and treatment. Many treatments are painful or their curative or even ameliorative affects unknown. The patient is the one who will suffer the pain or take the risk and so should be the one to make the ultimate decision. Sometimes, however, a patient does not want to be involved in decisions concerning his or her own care, or maybe wants to plan a future that in all likelihood may never happen. If so, that is the right and choice of the patient and we should honor it, as we would want our own decisions honored.

CHOICE

She was a little woman from Austria, now so thin and gaunt she could hardly weigh more than 80 pounds. She had not been outside her small apartment for almost two years, being tethered to her oxygen machine. The windows were covered with blinds, opened only slightly to let in some light, to distinguish day from night, but never open to take in the majesty of the mountains, the gigantic white clouds puffed against the azure sky. Maybe it was better not knowing. Maybe it was safe in this sealed space, her knowledge of the outside being carefully controlled by the daily brief sojourns of her husband to buy a few groceries, a newspaper, to do the laundry.

They were very exact, very precise, very neat. Everything in its place. Everything, maybe old, maybe tired, but immaculate. Perfect order.

One morning sitting in bed feeling especially weak, she told me about a friend who had liver cancer. My patient went to visit her friend, to keep her company, to help her pass the time – time that was coming to an end. Sitting next to her bedside with the afternoon sun casting warm shadows on the wall, the friend said –

"You know, my whole life I have always kept a perfect household. My linen closet was a reflection of the order I maintained. Everything folded uniformly, organized by color, by size. Now I wonder if it was all worth it, if it made any difference to anyone."

She told me nothing further about that incident, about that friend, about any thoughts she might have had listening to the sadness in her friend's voice. Instead she announced that this morning she made her husband clean all the kitchen cupboards, she had him take everything out, she had him wash the shelves with vinegar and water, then put everything back.

The friend's organized life mirrored her organized life. But unlike the friend she did not seem to question the value of her neat cupboards.

I have often wondered why she told me that story. Maybe she was saying "my friend questioned, but I do not want to go there. I want to hold on to my reality." That is her choice.

WISH AND HOPE

How does one have hope when facing death? Isn't hope an expectation of a future good? But when you are faced with imminent death, how can you feel there are real options? Where is the line between hope and a wish?

He was a brilliant man, educated and thoughtful. While his body was deteriorating, his mind stayed keen. Over the months I was with him we shared thoughts, views, opinions – politics, agriculture, religion, world events, local happenings. The intellectual exchange was stimulating and fun. We talked of the present, the past, but rarely, if ever, was there mention of the future – until one day.

It was a beautiful winter day where the sky is clear blue and despite the single digit temperature, you could feel the sun penetrate the cold. It spread a feeling of warmth over our faces. I had procured a wheelchair and as I pushed his bundled, emaciated body along the snowy path, we gloried in the blueness of the sky and the freshness of the air. Then he pointed to the hills and told me about his property.

It was situated in a small canyon farther up the road, slopes rising gently to each side, emptying south into the sunshine. He had owned it for some time and talked about it lovingly. Later when we returned home, he asked for some paper and a pencil. I brought it to him, and he began drawing. First he sketched in the canyon, the hills, and then his house. He had thought about its structure, its placement, its rooms, its functioning. He drew a floor plan for me, walking me through each room. This is what he was going to build on his land. There was no hesitancy in his statements, no dreamy glaze in his eyes. No if. No maybe. No hopefully. No acknowledgement of the limitations that his body was going to have on his plans.

I drove away that afternoon feeling a mixture of admiration and wonder. Did he really believe he would build his house? Was this a passion used to sustain him, the strength of positive thought which if truly believed would emerge into reality? Or were such musings employed to obscure the reality, to avoid any active thoughts of the future that actually awaited him? Was it a wish or a hope?

Maybe a little of both. Perhaps just sharing his dream made his day better.

TOMORROW

I had been reading to my patient when I looked up and saw her gazing out of the window.

"What are you thinking?" I asked.

"I was thinking about the fact that my house needs painting, but then I thought I'll do it next year." She was quiet for a moment, then looked at me and said, "How ridiculous is that? I won't be here next year."

Can she think about the future? What is the harm? And maybe she will be here next year. After all, last year she almost died. Her whole family flew in, surrounded her bed, and kept a vigil, but she chose to live. So who knows about tomorrow? By talking about projects for next year she is either exercising her right to be in denial, or she is planning for a tomorrow that may actually arrive.

THE RIGHT TO BE COMFORTABLE

The pain involved in dying is multifaceted. Although not all my pain can be taken away, please relieve whatever portion you can.

Nothing about dying is easy. No one should be required to demonstrate excessive bravery. If there is some medication or some therapy to ease the pain, the patient should have the right to receive it. Enduring pain is not ennobling. It is exhausting and mentally and physically debilitating. Drug addiction is not a concern of a dying person.

SILENCE

She was sitting in a wheelchair, slumped slightly to the right. Her right elbow rested on a sheepskin pad, her forearm was propped up, her head cradled in her hand. Her face was turned away, seemingly focused on the hollow space made by her bent arm. Her eyes were closed. The remains of her lunch sat on the table before her.

I introduced myself and my stated plan of taking her for a stroll in the sunshine. There was no glimmer of understanding. A nurse must have been feeding her since her arms appeared unmoving and her plate contained half eaten food. I picked up the spoon, scooped up a small bite of fruit and raised it to her lips. Her mouth, which lay slackly open, accepted the morsel and the jaw moved slowly up and down. It did not stop its movement despite the passage of sufficient time to consume that small bite. I held up the water filled glass and rested the straw between her lips. They gently softened around the straw and water ascended. I continued alternating the spoon and the straw, each action receiving a barely detectable response. Her eyes remained closed. I inquired if she was finished. I asked if she wanted more. There was no response or visible movement of her eyes, hands, head or body.

I pushed the dish away and removed the long bib that contained morsels of food that had dribbled from her mouth. I shifted the lever releasing the brake on her wheelchair and turned her toward the door and the sunshine.

It was a beautiful day. The ramp led down to an asphalt path that meandered around the grounds. As some points huge tree roots broke up through the pavement making it difficult to maneuver the wheelchair. Each passage over one of the bumps jolted the chair. She uttered no word or sound. Her eyes remained closed.

Sometimes I chatted – about the weather and the warmth of the sun and my hopes that this outing felt good. Other times I was silent, slowly pushing the wheel chair through the trees and over the grass. Sometimes I stopped next to a bench and sat, hoping she could feel the sun or the gentle winds that occasionally drifted through, sometimes commenting on the plants or flowers around us. Again no utterance, no movement, her head still resting in the palm of her right hand and her face still directed downward into the hollow.

Can she hear? Is she aware of her surroundings? Can she feel the sun? Is she imprisoned in a body that does not move but is cognizant of everything around? Or has her mind slipped into some no-man's land, some silent place that is peaceful and painless?

I felt such frustration. Was I helping her or hurting her? Did that jolting of the wheelchair send a pain through her body? I was reminded of the days when I had a one year old child. I did not know if his crying meant he was hungry or hurting or just plain tired. I used to say to him – if you could only talk to me, then I would know how to help you. I felt the same frustration now – "talk to me, tell me if I am helping or hurting you," were the words going through my mind.

It seemed that we had gone full circle. With her silence and inability to talk, like my one year old son, I did not know what was needed. I could only hope that she felt the warmth of the sun, that she smelled the freshness of the newly cut grass and the flowers along the path, that she felt the slight coolness of the wind, and that all of these things gave her some comfort.

PAIN

I remember the moment when I first saw him. He was sitting up in bed in a bright, sunny room – so handsome, so elegant, silver colored hair, piercing blue eyes and a wonderful smile – the picture of health. How could this man be dying of cancer? But he was, and over the months that followed, I saw the pain, and watched him wrestle, not just with the disease, but with issues of faith.

First there was the pain. Sometimes there were moments when the pain was so excruciating he would scream, a yell of such intensity that it pierced my body with the suddenness, strength and horror of an unseen arrow shot at point blank. It was the sound of terror. At one such moment he hurled his emaciated body across the bed, grabbing the pillow and burying his face in it, tears pooling into the pillowcase. "Why do I have such pain?" he wanted to know. "Why me?"

He had a friend, slightly older, who had died two weeks before. The friend had had no pain. Disease had riddled his friend's body, but it had closed down each function into a peaceful cessation of life. My patient was not so lucky. His pain was indescribable and unbearable. "There must be a reason for the pain," he whispered between sobs. He was a Christian Scientist so took no medication, but even medication at best dulls pain and provides only temporary relief. A reason? What could I tell him?

No one, whatever their beliefs, could suggest that his pain was some retribution for his past. He had lived a good life, been so caring and giving. He had been born in the country. As a young man with a wife and two children, he had been a rancher. One day he asked himself what he had done for mankind. He picked up his wife and children and joined the Peace Corps where they lived among and helped farmers and ranchers in South America. When he returned to this country, he became a teacher, stimulating discussion and urging his students to think and to work for a better environment. He worked with government officials to change laws to make conditions better for farmers and field laborers. He made a difference in many lives. He made the world a better place for his presence.

So why should he have such pain? I could have said, "you don't have to if you would let Hospice administer pain medication," but that would not be respectful of his belief system. I could only hold his hand.

THE RIGHT TO BE TOUCHED

Sometimes I need distance. Yet sometimes I have a strong need to be close. When I want to reach out, please come to me and hold me as I hold you.

The dying process is often one of slow mental and physical isolation. In life we may greet a friend with a warm hug, but now as the friend lays dying there is a hesitancy to touch. Often a patient is sick and frail, the skin is dry, the bones may be brittle. We may be concerned that a hug will hurt or cause a bruise, and so we do not touch. We may find the smell unpleasant so we create space between us. These things may be valid concerns or simply our explanation for keeping a distance, but they serve only to create further isolation. A kiss, a soft embrace, the resting of a hand on the hand of another creates a link and a suspension, even if momentary, of that sense of isolation. It is also a gift of love.

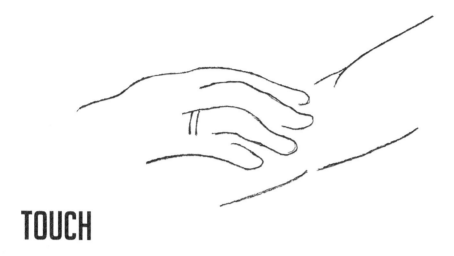

TOUCH

I must have been destined to be the one there at the end. It was my very first assignment as a Hospice volunteer. It was to be a very simple assignment – just sit with this woman who was not conscious while her husband took the dog for a walk and bought groceries. I did have to change a bandage, but otherwise that first afternoon was uneventful, except for the touch.

They had been married for a long time. Their 60th anniversary had likely long passed. He was a gentle, very quiet man. He walked slowly. She was bathed and dressed and made comfortable in a hospital bed which took up all the space in their small apartment living room. When he returned from his walk, he came straight to her. He touched her face. "Would you like some water?" he asked simply. There was no response, no indication that she even heard the soft, caring voice. He rubbed her arm so gently. He looked into her eyes though they were as opaque as clouded glass. He touched her face again and gently rubbed her head.

I felt honored to be in the presence of such love.

Though I was not scheduled to return the next day, I had time and offered to come. "How about 9:00?" I suggested. "No, I need to get her bathed and dressed first," he responded. "I can help you," I offered. "No, I want to do it. 10:00 will be fine."

The next morning the dog came to the door to greet me. I walked into the living room. He was sitting next to her. When he heard me, he stood only partially turning toward me, his eyes floating in tears. "She died 10 minutes ago," he whispered. I put my arms around him. Tears came to my eyes too. We sat next to each other and next to her, wet tissues filling our hands. We talked a little. I asked him to tell me about her. He got up and shuffled to the refrigerator where he took down a picture, handing it to me. A woman was riding a bike on the beach, a balloon trailing behind her. "We used to ride bikes and we camped. She loved flowers and balloons." He told me more about her. The quiet was warm and comfortable and so peaceful. I felt privileged once more, being in that room filled with gentle love and a lifetime of unspoken memories. Mostly I remember his touch.

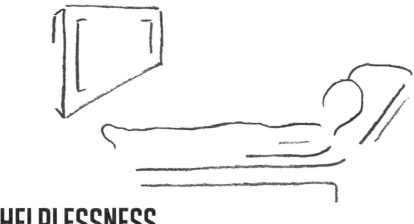

HELPLESSNESS

It should have been an easy afternoon for me. He had ALS, that horrible, slowly paralyzing disease that pulls all life from your body while leaving your brain intact. He could not move or speak, and spent his waking hours lying propped in a hospital bed in front of a huge television. He likes action movies, I was told, and that's what he was watching when I arrived.

I stood at the head of his bed. For over an hour I massaged his head, neck and shoulders. There were no words, but he could move his head partially from side to side. As he rolled his head against my palm or turned away laying open the other side of his neck for attention, I knew I was giving him pleasure. The movie continued. I moved to his hands, pulling each finger, gently kneading my fists into his palms. His eyes continued to focus on the TV, but he seemed relaxed. Then the movie ended.

The next film on the channel was an animated cartoon, not something I thought would be of interest to him. I picked up the remote control and pushed the button for a different channel. Oh no! Fuzz, then nothing, then fuzz again. The buttons – I kept pushing them. There were three remote control devices on the table next to his bed. I tried each one. Still nothing. I pushed the buttons on the TV itself – off and blank. Panic! This is his life, what am I to do! I'm apologizing profusely, but that is no consolation. He's probably wondering what kind of person Hospice has sent – I can feed him, massage him, clean him, but I can't work his TV – the one mechanical thing so crucial to his existence.

Finally in desperation I called his caregiver. She was in another city for the day. I had never met her. She was wonderful. She walked me through each step on the controls. Finally, a picture – a cops and robbers show. Perfect. I sighed and relaxed. Back in control.

While his eyes focused on this new adventure show, I pulled up a chair next to his bed and picking up a newspaper settled into an interesting article. His body seemed peaceful. I relaxed. Then it started.

He was a man who could not speak and could not move. Yet from his throat came horrible, gut wrenching sobs. Tears poured profusely from his eyes, mucous ran from his nose. But it was the sound that I remember – sheer agony and pain, deep from within, and it did not stop. I wiped his face. I put my arms around his shoulders. Nothing seemed to help. I repeated over and over – "it will be alright" – though nothing could be further from the truth. Why did I say that? What should I say? Has this happened before? No one had told me, not even the volunteer who had been with him, seeing him several times a week for over a year. I wondered – did my massage, my touch, release all of this from within?

His mind could think, his body could feel, but he could not move, he could not touch, he could not communicate. Total helplessness. And there I was, in a different state of helplessness. I could move, I could talk, but there was nothing I could do to help him, to ease his torment. I could only hold him.

THE RIGHT TO LAUGHTER

People often – for too often – come to me wearing masks of seriousness. Although dying, I still need to laugh. Please laugh with me and help others to laugh as well.

So many people walk into a sick room as if they were preparing for a funeral. The situation is grave, so too they believe, must be their demeanor. Clearly there is nothing fun about dying, but until we are dead, we are alive, and part of living is laughter. Laughter is not a denial of reality. Rather it provides a momentary suspension of pain and the negatives of one's situation. It is a gift of life.

HELPING

My Hospice patient and I laugh a lot, especially as we work together on this book. She has a terrific sense of humor. The other day when we were discussing a patient's right to laughter, she said, "That reminds me...." and she told me the following story:

> My friend B was dying and I went over to see her. I had recently had a problem with my hip and my Achilles heel and I was not walking very well and only short distances and with a cane. I hobbled in through the kitchen and into the living room where she was now resting in a hospital bed. She was no longer going out and her days were now confined to this room and this bed. I asked her if there was anything I could do for her. She thought only a moment and said she would love it if I read to her.
>
> "Oh dear," I said. "I'm sorry B but my eyesight is not very good. I can't even read to myself anymore. Is there something else I can do for you?"

"Well," she said. "There are some letters I would like to write. Would you write them for me?"

"Oh dear," I said again. "I'm afraid my Parkinson's makes my good hand shake so that I don't think anyone would be able to read anything I wrote. Is there something else I can do for you?"

She thought a minute and said, "My poor dog has been so cooped up. It would be wonderful if you could take him for a walk."

At that moment we both looked at my cane and burst out laughing. What a pair we were! I thought all I could really do was crawl into bed with her. We could not stop laughing."

It was the best present she could have given her friend.

DESSERT

It was the end. Her youngest daughter flew in from San Francisco. Her older sister, not in great health herself, immediately boarded a plane. Even her former husband made the trek across the country. Their divorce many years ago had devastated her, but time softens memories and age shortens distances. He was lonely and not ready to deal with loss of the friendship regenerated in recent years through long distance telephone calls. The two oldest daughters lived nearby so their frequent visits changed to longer vigils.

She had been tethered to an oxygen machine for many months, but the long flexi cord allowed freedom to meander around her house and sit in her garden on warm summer days. Now she did not move from her bed. She dozed for long periods, wakened by pain and then sent back to the edges of oblivion through the mercy of morphine. A heavy silence filled the house like a San Francisco fog, broken periodically by soft whispers here and there or the peaceful chanting of her Buddhist daughter. A Hospice nurse hovered, an IV was hooked up. Hydration and morphine seeped slowly through the clear line. The grandchildren came. Granny was dying. Then suddenly, she wasn't.

She had started out as my Hospice patient. I was supposed to read to her several hours a week as her eyesight could no longer distinguish facial features much less that oversized print in the books her friends had given her. But her brain was still fascinated with life. Every subject interested her – politics, global warming, the wars and slaughter in the middle east, and even local council meetings which often generated lively debate. When current events were exhausted, she delved into Catholicism with its child molestation lawsuits, the religious right with the hypocrisy of many of its leaders, and her understanding and embrace of Buddhist philosophy. She had thoughtful opinions on everything and loved to ruminate on the future of the world. Even alien life was a topic of discussion. The time passed so quickly that I started coming an extra day so we could finish some of those books she wanted to read.

I knew days were limited with my new friend, but for several hours two days a week, we lived in the moment. Then just when that moment appeared final, it wasn't.

I got the news and joyfully drove to her home. She was sitting up in bed, a silk scarf resting softly over her shoulders, her eyes welcoming. As I walked into the room she looked up at me and said, "Now what?" She had been ready. She told me she had seen people standing around her bed, unknown people, waiting. She did not feel any sense of fear from these people. She knew they were waiting for her, and she was ready. Then she woke up. What had they given her in those IV tubes? She had been so afraid of dying in a desert, dry, parched, her lips desiccated, her body aching for a drop of water. The image haunted her so she had checked that box on the "Final Wishes" paper that said no food, just morphine and hydration. She did not know that as her organs closed down one by one she would slip quietly, she would not feel any raging thirst. She did not know that with hydration her body could be sustained for a long time, that she could even wake up, come back. She had been ready. But now she was back. "Now what?"

We chatted. Then her caregiver came in and asked what she would like for lunch. Soup? Sandwich? Fruit? "No," she said, "just some of Shirley's noodle pudding." "Nothing else?" "No, just noodle pudding." Dessert.

Then her sister walked in. She was on her way home, saying goodbye for now.

"Now dear, it's important that you eat. You need to gain weight. You need to eat healthful food, lots of fruits and vegetables. I also want you to get some exercise. Go back to those water aerobics. They were good for you. You need to get some muscle tone and strength back. Getting up, walking. These are important."

Lunch was brought in - noodle pudding, with a generous side of grapes and mangoes and some whole wheat toast.

Her sister stayed a while longer, then with a hug and one more reminder about food and exercise, she left. I walked back in. The grapes and mangoes and toast were untouched. The noodle pudding was gone.

"I know the answer to your question, " I said.

"What question?" she asked.

"What now?" I said.

"Oh?"

"Eat dessert!"

We both laughed. Yes, and lots of laughter.

THE RIGHT TO CRY AND EXPRESS ANGER

It is difficult to leave behind all my attachments and all that I love. Please allow me the opportunity to be sad and angry.

While one does not want to dwell on all the attachments one is leaving behind, they should not be dismissed lightly. The loss is there. It is heavy. It is a hole in one's heart. It is part of life and must be allowed a voice.

CONTROL

"He's being mean to me. He's malicious and he's just spiteful." These were the first words my patient said to me when I walked in that afternoon.

"What did he do to you?" I asked gently.

"He plopped a half an orange on top of my salad. It was not cut up and he knows I can't eat it like that."

Spiteful? Malicious? What harsh words to describe what appeared to me to be simply not thinking. After all, she had always done the cooking. Even in her greatly debilitated state in which she was forced to rely more on him each day, and to relinquish bit by bit her control of meal preparation, he could never quite do it right. Too much, not enough. Did you get out the steamer? How much water did you put in it? Did you turn it on? How hot? No, turn it down. Don't turn it on yet.

You know he wasn't intending to be spiteful when he topped the salad with a half an orange, but what to say to her? He's in his 80's and struggling in the kitchen. This is hard for him. She was always so competent, such a great cook.

"He's so mean," she says. But I think to myself – he's crying inside, he's losing the one he loves. How can I help her see this and not view his conduct as "mean"?

Each day as we get closer to her death, the tension is increasing.

"We fought all night, and he yells at me and he's crabby all the time," she tells me one morning.

"I'm not crabby," he yells, obviously having overheard our conversation from the next room. Later when I was with him in the kitchen he said to me, "I'm sorry I was rude."

"Rude? You weren't rude," I tell him.

"But she tells me all the time that I'm rude to you."

"No, you are not," I assure him. He, the caretaker, the husband, the one who will be left behind, is getting exhausted. The other Hospice volunteer and I try to get him out, take walks, see friends, get away. But it's hard for him to do. There is something in him that insists he be there to the end. Yet without being able to replenish himself, it is making the end so difficult, so tense. And she is so strong, holding on long past where others would have left.

I am reminded of something I learned in our Hospice training – as we become older, we become more of what we are, and we go out as we have lived. I have only known her for about a year, but she has struck me as a person who prefers living in a set routine. She was raised in Europe. She is a person who wants to be in control, for whom trust is difficult because it is a relinquishment of control, who is very demanding, having meticulous standards for herself and expecting the same in others.

But in death we leave routine. We must learn to trust, especially as all of our bodily functions begin to require assistance from others. We can no longer control and must let go. Intellectually she knows this, but she is fighting to the end, attempting to dictate and control as she has done in life. Leaving as she has lived. If he could understand this, understand that her anger is not really directed at him but at the diminishing control she has over her life, it might be easier and might not hurt as much.

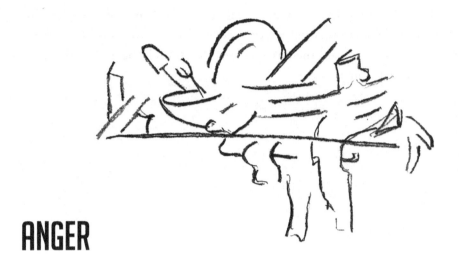

ANGER

He had married later in life. His wife was quite a bit younger and they had two young daughters. He had worked in an industry that provided a jet set life – traveling first class to places all around the world, hobnobbing with all the rich and famous. Now however, he was dying and they were living in a condo in a little mountain town. His wife opened the door and showed me into the guest room where he now resided. He was in a big bed surrounded by rumpled sheets, blankets and pillows. The dresser and chair that barely fit in the room were covered with books, papers, dishes, cups, playthings for the girls. No surface was bare.

Since I was to bathe him, shave him and give him lunch, his wife took me down the short hall into the kitchen. Everywhere there were clothes, some left on the floor, but most hanging on portable racks, chair backs, any protruding object, in order to dry. She must have felt self-conscious or noticed my eyes taking in the scene because as we walked by she volunteered, "I don't like using a dryer."

The kitchen was equally chaotic. Dishes were piled in the sink, overflowing on to counters. The kitchen table and every available surface were piled with papers – bills, junk mail, magazines, no particular order, everything stacked haphazardly, not little piles, but stacks at least a foot high or more. She opened the refrigerator, equally crammed, and suggested a few things I might make him for lunch. Then she took the girls and left.

He did not say much through the bathing process, and while I had had little experience shaving men, I managed to complete the job without any nicks requiring dobs of Kleenex. Once dressed and back in bed, with lunch on his lap, he started to talk.

"She just married me for the money and the lifestyle," he informed me. "Now she doesn't want to touch me or have anything to do with me. She just wants to know when the next check is coming or when my royalties will arrive." It is amazing what people will tell complete strangers when facing their own mortality.

Things did not change over the next weeks. Clothes were perpetually drying. Paper stacks did not diminish, and the complaints were reiterated and expanded. There were no indications of affection between the husband and wife, no touches, no inquiries as to how he felt or where she was going. She did tell me one day that there was no way she would bathe her husband, that was not something she could do.

It was the first time I had been in such an angry unhappy environment. You think that facing death, knowing there is a finite time together, a limited number of days to coexist, that a special reserve could be drawn upon to show some caring, some concern. But sometimes the dying process is just too difficult to handle. One only wonders if when the end comes, will there be any regret.

THE RIGHT TO EXPLORE THE SPIRITUAL

Whether I am questioning or affirming, doubting or praising, I sometimes need your ear, a nonjudgmental ear. Please let my spirit travel its own journey, without judging its direction.

Near the end of life, there is the obvious question – "what next" -- and all of the attendant emotions that go with the inquiry. Some have a strong belief in a religion that provides an answer. Others do not. Even despite a belief in a blissful hereafter, there often remains uncertainty and unarticulated fear.

Because of our societal timidity concerning the subject of death, this is one area where patients may need help beginning the conversation. The subject can be raised by simple questions concerning disposition of their physical remains and how they would like their family and friends to celebrate their lives. From there a gentle inquiry into the patient's belief may provide an opportunity to talk about fears and hopes, and help the caregiver provide comfort, directly or through the assistance of others, when thinking about "what next."

FACING DEATH

"I almost died last night, but I didn't." Those were the first words she said to me as I sat down in the chair next to her bed. "Tell me about it," I said.

"I was right there, but I couldn't go across." After a moment she added, "My daughter is in Paris with her boyfriend. I didn't want to ruin her vacation."

"What was it like?" I asked.

"There was pressure holding me. It was like the time I was on the Concorde, when we went through the sound barrier. There is a feeling of pressure, and then you are through. It's quiet. But I could not breathe."

"How were you feeling," I asked.

There was a long silence, her face tightening, her eyes blank, sad. Finally she said, "I felt lost."

"Was it lost as in you didn't know where you were or which way to go? Was it lost as in being all alone? Was it lost as in being afraid?"

"I was afraid," she whispered. "All my Buddhist beliefs were gone. I had nothing to believe. I didn't know what would be there."

About nine months before she had come close to death. At that time she saw people standing next to her bed, not moving, not talking, faceless, just waiting. She felt they were there for her. She did not feel fear. This time however she was alone and afraid.

Tears then came to her eyes as she said to me, "I am using up what should be my children's." I knew what she was trying to say – by staying alive, by having 24 hour a day caregivers, whatever assets she had would be dissipated and her children would not receive any inheritance upon her death.

What to say to her? I could only imagine the thoughts going through her mind – "I am taking up space with a life that is physically limited, that is using up the assets I have, that is preventing me from making any gifts to my daughters – all because I am afraid, afraid to leave, afraid of what is on the other side, of what is after this world. Why should I be afraid? But I am. Why? Where is the Buddhist philosophy I have held for so long? Why is it not there for me? Why am I afraid?"

What could I tell her? About using her daughters' inheritance, all I could say was, "Do not think that way." But that is no consolation. How can I tell her not to be afraid? I have not faced that wall, that void, that pressure. I don't know what I would feel. I cannot tell her what to feel or what not to feel. I cannot give her faith or bring back the faith she had. I could only hold her hand and listen.

DUST

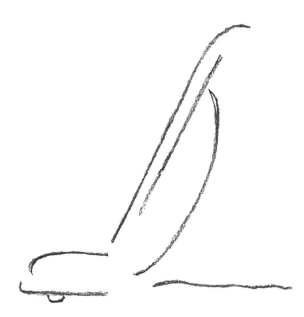

There had been so many months of talking and reading and laughing that I was not prepared for the thin, weak voice on the telephone that said, "I am not feeling well today, and am not up to having you read to me, but you may come to see me." She was dying. While I intellectually knew this, for she was my Hospice patient, the hours of lively debate, discussion of current events, and sharing of past experiences, had pushed this knowledge into the recesses of my mind. This was my new friend. We had so many more books to read, more memories to share. She could not leave yet. But she was, and she was telling me to come.

During my prior visit, she had slept. I sat next to her, holding her hand, gently stroking her arm, sending love, believing she could feel it, willing any pain to leave and let her body rest. But this time she was sitting at the table radiant in her pink dressing gown, drinking tea from her white porcelain cup.

"Good morning, pretty lady," I said, and received a most beautiful smile. The Hospice nurse was sitting next to her, having come for her daily check.

Turning to the Hospice nurse she said, "Thank you for asking about what I wanted and for the priest you sent me, knowing about my Catholic upbringing."

I knew about her Catholicism as a child, for we had both shared it. We used to call up memories of the nuns who taught us, with their flowing robes and stiff head dresses allowing only a small circle of eyes, nose and mouth to appear to the public. Did they have hair under there – an apparently universal question for pubescent girls. We had both seen the discriminating treatment of nuns in those days – women who taught school, spent hours in church and who did all the housekeeping and cooking for the priests, tethered to their rectory, while the priests drove the latest model cars provided by their parishioners, played golf, and imbibed frequently while being invited to family dinners. At least that is what we observed from our adolescent viewpoints, and that was long before the pedophile scandals rocked the church.

She had left that religion behind, while at the same time acknowledging values it had given her. She had been pulled toward Buddhism – the simplicity, the honesty, the awareness. One of her daughters practiced Buddhism and sometimes as I walked up the stairs to the main floor I would hear the deep, haunting beautiful sounds of her chanting.

After the Hospice nurse left I asked her about the priest's visit. "The priest was nice," she said. "He agreed to preside over everything. I did not want to be dust." She pointed her finger in the air. "Dust. There's me." She pointed at another spot, "There's me," and then another, and another, each time repeating, "There's me. Dust." She did not want to be dust, to be floating in space, to be vacuumed. She wanted to be encapsulated, all in one piece, safe in the ground.

She had been close to death once before. She remembered it. It had been so easy with the pills. It was dark and warm, a gentle floating down. Peaceful. Nothing to fear. The darkness would just close around her, a soft plush blanket, warming her into sleep. So easy, comforting.

I had believed her vision. I had believed she was not afraid to die, that death was just a passage. But now on the edge, a new thought arose – dust. She did not want to be dust, did not want to disappear into the air. I who thought I knew her, never guessed this concern, this fear. We had talked about so many things, but never her "final arrangements." Had I assumed she had taken care of this, or had I assumed it was not important? Whatever it was, I had made assumptions. She said over and over that she was ready to go. But perhaps we are never truly ready. Despite our beliefs and our faith, the end of the known holds all of us in some way, even if for only a moment, even if only by the thought of dust.

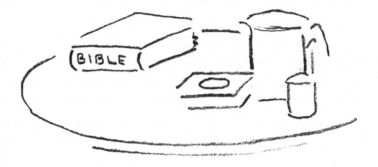

HEARING

In our Hospice training we are told the importance of listening. It is not just to provide an ear, a presence, a body to dispel the sense of aloneness, though sometimes that is a very important function of our work. Sometimes we can only help if we truly listen.

There was an older woman lying in extreme pain. She was devoted to her Bible. It was next to her at all times. She read from it every day, or when she was too weak to pick it up, a friend would read to her. The words were water for her life.

The Hospice nurse had procured medication to relieve some of her pain. The pills remained on her table, next to her Bible, but were not touched, not used. When questioned about the nonuse, the woman informed the nurse that her Bible told her not to use pain relievers, that her suffering was God's will and that intervention through medication would thwart that will.

The nurse listened and then offered the following suggestion. "I know your Bible is important to you, that you read its pages every day. As your disease progresses you may find it difficult to hold the book or even to focus on the words. We have the Bible on tape and perhaps you would like to listen to it, and while you listen you may hear words that tell you it is alright to take action to lessen some of your pain."

The next day the woman turned on the tape machine, and she took her medicine. She had been allowed to maintain her faith without compromising her religious beliefs. It was only by listening to her spiritual needs that the nurse was able to provide for her physical ones.

THE RIGHT TO HAVE A SENSE OF FAMILY

No matter what defines my present family – it may be a small circle of friends and caregivers, it may encompass relatives or not – I have need, now more than ever, to experience the connectedness, the intimacy, and the interdependence that constitute family.

As a patient's life becomes more physically circumscribed and isolated, it is even more important to feel connected. The connection may be provided by family members, relatives, friends or caregivers. It is a connection with those we love and who love us. Most patients have a fear that at the end they will die in pain and alone. With Hospice care there is no need to die in pain. If the patient is surrounded by those who love him, he will not die alone.

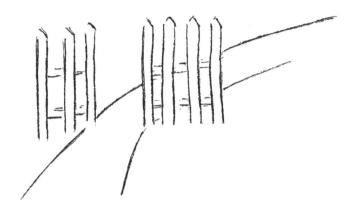

DEPARTURE

When I walked into her bedroom I knew she was going to leave on my watch. She was in her late 80's, her diminutive body almost disappearing in the expansiveness of the hospital bed. There were bars on the side of the bed to keep her from falling, though it was apparent that it would have taken an exertion nowhere in her body to even reach across the ocean of sheets to merely touch the cold metal. Her eyes were closed, her face softened, wrinkles gently furrowed like a dormant winter field. Life beneath, quiet, almost imperceptible, except for the breaths – hoarse, raspy, almost painful to the ears.

I remembered that sound. It was the sound that came from my husband that last night before he died. It came from deep within, harsh, heavy, gurgling, rolling up, out. An awful noise, scary, again and again. Only later did I hear it called a death rattle. What an apt description.

So when I walked into her room and heard that sound, I knew she was getting ready to leave. Her daughter, patient, kind, her caregiver, was going out for a walk, for air, for space. That was another reason I knew. I have learned that people who are dying often wait until they are alone. They choose the moment when the last family member goes out of the room.

That person may have left to get a sandwich, to make a call or to use the bathroom. It can only be a matter of minutes, but that is often when they choose to leave.

It is not a cruelty, but a last gift to those they love, sparing them the pain of that moment of finality. However, when you have been waiting by the bed, waiting vigilantly for hours, days, months, to be there at the end, to assure them that you are with them, it's upsetting when the one you love leaves without you, waits for the one moment you are not there. It does not feel like a gift at the time. It might even feel selfish. Maybe it is. Then again, maybe it's an act of courage on the part of the person dying, a statement that dying is something we have to do alone, and that by leaving alone the person is saying "it's okay, I am alright, you may now go on living."

I knew from the sound and the departure of her daughter that she was making this choice. I held her hand. I told her it was okay, she could leave, and "when you get there, say hello to my love for me." I don't know whether these souls will meet, but sometimes you pass on the message even if it may never reach its destination.

A few minutes later her breathing changed. It stopped. "That's it," I thought. Just one second from there to not there. Then another breath, a few, irregular, then nothing. Two seconds, four seconds, ten seconds – who knows how long as I held still, waiting, listening, watching, wondering if I had just heard the last one. Another breath, silence, seemingly shorter this time. She's not ready to go. I continued to hold her hand. I relaxed. Then I realized, there was no sound, no movement. I waited. I waited. I breathed slowly, consciously. My breaths were not matched. There were no more.

And she gave me a gift, for I was the one there when her daughter returned. I got to hold her daughter. I got to tell her it was okay, that her mother had wanted it this way.

THINGS I HAVE LEARNED FROM MY HOSPICE PATIENTS

There are many things I have learned from my Hospice patients that are not embodied neatly under the concepts articulated in the patient's bill of rights. Some I have learned from other caregivers, some from watching and listening to my patients.

ABOUT LEAVING

I have learned from my Hospice patients that each of us chooses the time to leave. It may be a time when one is surrounded by family and friends, or it may be a time when one is alone. It is a personal choice and those left behind need not say, "if only I hadn't….left the room, or gone to lunch, or accepted that call, or run that errand, or taken an earlier plane."

That last week of my husband's life was difficult. We were packing and planning to move to our small vacation home in the mountains, 850 miles away. I was exhausted. I had just climbed into bed next to my husband and had fallen asleep instantly. In what felt like one minute my son woke me to tell me my husband, his dad, had just died.

For years I remembered that moment and kept chastising myself. Why had I fallen asleep? Why couldn't I have waited another minute? Why did he leave me like that? For years that moment weighed on me. I felt somehow deficient in my love, in my caregiving, in that I was not there at the moment he left. That one moment of sleep haunted me.

Since then I have learned both in my Hospice training and from my patients that I need not have felt that way, that it was my husband's choice. It was not meant to cause me hurt. It may even have been to spare me pain. A few hours after he died the movers arrived to pack up our things and take us to the place that had always held happy memories for all of us. Those memories would not be clouded with death or sorrow. I now understand that leaving at that moment was my husband's last gift to me and those he loved.

LEAVING

He died Saturday night. He waited for his son to come to be with him, but then he chose a moment in the middle of the night, alone, to leave.

Had he heard the conversation between his son and the Hospice nurse? Did he hear his son say that he could not take it anymore, that he could not just sit there and watch his father die? Could he feel his son's anxiety, sense his fear and his inability to deal with death? Did he know that his son had called the airline, that he had moved up his departure and that he was now planning to leave early Sunday morning rather than stay through the whole weekend as originally planned? Did he hear the son say he couldn't watch it anymore, that he had to get away, that his father would be alright alone, that the neighbors and Hospice would look in, that this would be enough, that if he died alone between those visits, it would be okay? Did he hear these statements? Was it okay? Were all of these thoughts in his consciousness when he slipped into bed that Saturday night?

He was a handsome man – tall, athletic with that grey hair that in men makes them look distinguished. He had become ill just before Christmas when he was diagnosed with stomach cancer. It was a shock. The cancer was growing rapidly. His stomach had become distended. He looked as if he were pregnant, carrying a new life, not a growth that was extinguishing one. There was no treatment. He accepted the pronouncement of his doctor and settled into his chair, waiting to die.

He had been a golfer. It was his love, his passion, his life. He had been one of the founders of the golf course near his house. He was happy telling me about those early days when they assembled the land, met with course architects and designers, worked with the city through the lengthy process of obtaining approvals. He had been involved in and had watched the construction and completion of the first 18 holes. They were now working on the development of another 9 holes. He was alive when he talked about his golf course. But it was now blanketed in snow, the grass not dead, just dormant, just waiting for the spring, for the warmth, for a new life.

I wanted him to hold on, to be able to experience one more spring, to be able to sit and take in once more the lush green fairways, the white sand and the sparkling water, and to feel the sun on his face. We were almost there. The weather had turned warm, the snow was melting rapidly. The last time I saw him I told him we would take a short walk, go outside and I would bring a wheel chair to make it easier.

He knew the spring was coming, the time of the year he had always loved. But he also knew this year would be different. He would not walk those links, he would not swing his club, he would not tee up a ball. These things were concrete, undeniable evidence that his life here was coming to an end. Were these thoughts in his mind Saturday night when he lay down in his bed and pulled his covers up to his chin?

It had been a relatively good life – a career in real estate, primarily managing projects for a bank. He talked animatedly about those times, the hurdles he faced, the places he traveled, the men he worked with. In those early days he had had a wife and two children. There was a divorce and now it seemed no significant connection with those grown children or their families. He had had a second wife, two more children, one of whom died in a fire after a short life. The other son was the only one left, the only one who came, the one to whom he was now bequeathing his estate, the one who could not watch his father die, who could not be there.

So he chose his moment – the last moment the son could be there but not with him, not watching, not experiencing that second he took leave. He knew that would be too hard for his son. And he chose the moment before the sun and sky and green grass could call him outside and remind him of what he was leaving. He went quietly, alone, at a moment he chose.

ABOUT LISTENING

One of the most important things I have learned is that we need to listen and not impose our beliefs on others, especially those in pain or facing death. We do it in simple ways without even realizing it and with the best of intentions. We tell them they should get up and walk around as they will feel better. We tell them they should eat more, especially fruits and vegetables because it will give them strength. We tell them what we think they should do, what we believe is best for them.

But is that really what they want? Will more fruits and vegetables really improve the quality of their lives? Are those facing imminent death really worried about what another cigarette will do to their lungs? Are those in extreme pain really worried about becoming addicted to morphine?

When we insist that a patient eat more and we succeed in getting that homemade chicken soup down a stomach, it may make us feel better as we are "doing something." But did that patient really want the chicken soup? Would she have preferred chocolate? We need to listen.

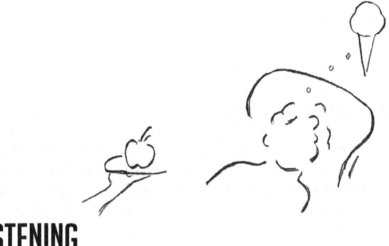

LISTENING

She was dying – only days or perhaps hours from the end. At least that is what I felt when I walked into the room. I needed to clean her up a bit and change her pants, actually a diaper. Isn't it strange how many of us will depart in the same clothes that we wore when we first arrived in this world? The same clothes and the same helplessness. I was told the family did not want to do these things. I wondered why it was different from infancy, at least from the perspective of the caregiver.

I needed to roll her sideways to be able to pull the diaper out from under her body and to clean her well. However, every time I touched her, she moaned. The pain, that awful pain. How can I do this quickly and cause the least amount of pain. It wasn't the best job, but I chose to trade a modicum of hospital worthy cleanliness for comfort and cessation of pain. I covered her and held her hand, rubbing it gently, wondering if that touch, no matter how lovingly given, was itself causing pain. Then in came a friend.

"Has she had anything to eat?" the friend demanded of me without introduction or any words of greeting.

"No," I replied. "Her husband said that she had had some tea earlier."

The friend then announced, "We must get some broth in her. I will make it."

A few minutes later the friend returned, soup bowl and spoon in hand. Standing over the patient, she maintained a constant chatter – weather, activities, people she had seen – punctuated with commands to "open your mouth" as she thrust the spoon forward, reminiscent of a doctor wielding a tongue depressor. Each time, barely conscious, her eyes closed, the patient would comply, as the broth was spooned into her mouth, sometimes overflowing down her chin to an awaiting washcloth. "We have to get all this broth down you, and then change your sheets, and we'll roll you around which will stimulate your bladder." Oh dear, I thought. That did not sound comfortable.

A short time into the feeding process, a Hispanic housekeeper arrived. "Come in here," the friend called to the housekeeper. Then in an authoritative, take charge manner, she said to the housekeeper, motioning with her head toward the patient, "Speak to her in Spanish."

"But what shall I say?" the housekeeper asked shyly.

"Talk to her about the weather, ask her questions. It doesn't matter. It's important that she talk, and speaking in Spanish will help stimulate her brain."

The housekeeper complied. The patient mumbled a few words in a halting manner, suggesting she was having difficulty with the effort involved in simply speaking, much less in a non-native language. Finally the effort became too much and the patient whispered, "I don't want to speak Spanish. It's too hard."

The friend finally conceded, but only on this subject. She persevered regarding the soup.

"You must get food in you. You must get perky. Your sons are coming." It was Christmas and the sons were returning, presumably knowing it would be the last visit with their mother.

The soup task finally completed, the friend then asked, "Now, what do you want to eat? You must have something. How about an avocado? I'll have your husband call his friend at the restaurant to make sure we get a perfect avocado for you."

Maybe inappropriately I then asked in a pleading voice, "Can we just let her rest a while?"

"Alright," the friend responded. "We'll let her sleep for 15 minutes before we change her linens." I did not want to think of the pain that would cause her, especially rolling her around "to stimulate her bladder."

As I walked away that afternoon, I wondered why we cannot let the dying die. Why did she have to eat? Why did she have to be "perky"? Why did she have to consume liquids that her body would then have to deal with? Why can we not listen to the patient? It pained me so. I felt so powerless, an interloper. I was not family or close friend. I know they were all there to help and certainly meant well, but I wanted to scream – stop! Leave her in peace. Does it matter if her sheets are not immaculate? Should we be more concerned about the cleanliness of the linens than the pain that would be inflicted by moving her to change those sheets? What is important? I know this friend was trying to help, and indeed perceived her actions as such. But whom was she helping? We need to learn to listen.

ABOUT LIFE

Facing the end of life on this earth there is a temptation to look back and ask "what if....", to remember the decisions one made and wonder about the roads not taken, or to express regret and think only "I wish I had....".

We can help those facing the end turn from these negative thoughts and reminisce instead about the things they did and the experiences they had.

LIFE LIVED

Strange things started happening to him. He was only in his late 60's, in good physical shape and quite active. He was an artist, welding huge sculptures of steel and bronze, exertions requiring great strength and precision. Then he would drive into town to go shopping and while standing in line with groceries scanning through the conveyor belt, discover he did not have his wallet. Or he would arrive in town and not remember why he was there. Or he would go out into the parking lot and forget which car was his. Little things. Little memory lapses.

When these blanks began to increase he went to the city for tests. There he got the news – a brain tumor, not operable. He chose to come home and wait for the end.

I had known him for over 20 years. He had not married and had had no children. We were friends. We had hiked, and fished and talked over coffee and shared picnics. Now he sat quietly in his chair.

"May I ask you something?" I inquired.

"Of course," he said.

"Now that you are at the end of your physical life here, and as you look back on your life, is there anything you wish you had done?"

He thought for a moment and then said, "No. I have had a wonderful life."

As I walked away that day I thought how incredibly lucky he was. How many of us can say that? How many of us say, "I wish I had...I should have...If I could only do it over again." How many of us can say, "I have had a wonderful life."

ABOUT GRIEVING

There is no right or wrong way to grieve. For some tears come instantly and often, for some tears come not at all, or at some unexpected time, maybe even years later. Some want to be surrounded by family and friends at the time of their loss. Some want to be alone. It is important to ask. The last thing we want is to make the grieving person feel "guilty" because they are not expressing their grief in a particular way. There is no protocol for grief.

CRYING

We spent the morning on her patio – the sun so lovely, the umbrella providing shade, and the ice tea sweet and cool. After a lively political discussion she was tired and decided to return to her room to rest. I got her settled with her white stuffed bunny curled around her head, and as I leaned over to give her a hug and tell her I would see her Monday, she looked up at me and said, "I still haven't cried."

Her older sister, who until six month ago, had been in good health and actively flying between her home in southern California, her grandchildren in Florida, and our little mountain town where she had a second home, had died four weeks ago. In the fall her sister had been diagnosed with cancer. She was determined to beat it and had undergone chemotherapy and radiation, with all the attendant side effects. Upon completion of her therapy, the tests revealed that treatment had not been 100% successful, and the cancer had spread to her brain and back. In less than three weeks, she was gone – her older sister, the one who was healthy, the one to whom she talked almost every day. She was gone. Despite the closeness, the caring, the love, and the extreme loss, my patient had not cried.

Do we have to cry when we lose someone we love? Is there a schedule for crying? Are we in some way defective, uncaring, if we do not cry? This was her sister, her only sibling. Of course they had had their rivalries in younger years, but there was always love, and years had brought a new kind of closeness. Her sister was her family and now she was gone. Why could she not cry?

"I did not cry until four years after my husband died," I told her. I remember that day so clearly. I had been to the funeral of an associate. I came home, pulled out all the pictures and letters and everything I had received and kept and thrown in a box at the time of my husband's death. I spent the afternoon crying, going through each item, reading, reminiscing, crying – big huge tears falling in my lap, loud sobs. I had had two young sons when my husband died and I knew I had to keep everything together for them. But that is no reason for not crying. I could have cried at night, alone, in my bed. But I hadn't. I didn't cry until that day four years later when I came home from a friend's funeral.

We know the importance of crying and its therapeutic effects, but it comes at its own time. It can be immediate. It can be months after the body has been laid to rest. It can be years. There is no schedule, no "right" time. Maybe for some it never comes. But when and if it comes, it is so healing. Until then, it is okay not to cry.

ABOUT LITTLE CONNECTIONS

As we go about our busy days, living actively – with jobs, children, vacations, friends – it's easy to forget that many do not have such full lives. Their bodies have begun to fail and daily routines have narrowed in scope and place, so that they no longer can be fully included in our lives. We still love them and still think about them, but they cannot feel our thoughts. They can only feel as if they are disappearing. It does not take much time, but a short email, a telephone call, a card – make a difference and last longer in the memory of our patient, friend or family member than the time it took to do that little thing.

THE INVITATION

My Hospice patient and I have a common friend who often throws big parties in her country home. My patient has known her friend for many years and has always been included in any soiree, particularly the large, cocktail party where my patient can find a centrally located chair and easily visit with all. At her own annual Christmas party she holds court on her hearth which is boldly set in the middle of her living room.

I had just received an invitation to a private concert in our friend's back yard. A pianist would be performing wonderful, light show tunes and classical love songs. It was a summer celebration of life and song in memory of a man who brought so much music to our mountain town. I was looking forward to it.

My patient looked at me sadly. "I didn't get invited," she said.

"Perhaps the hosts felt it would be too strenuous for you, and they know you rarely go out of your home these days," I proffered, hoping to lessen her sadness.

Looking at me straight in the eyes, she said, "I couldn't have gone, but it's nice to have the option to decline."

At that moment I realized something more significant had happened. She had been forgotten. In going through the list of potential invitees, the hosts had undoubtedly seen her name for she had been in their lives a long time and they had faithfully attended her Christmas parties. But this time they scanned past, knowing, as she herself admitted, she would not accept the invitation, so why send one? The hosts' reaction was so understandable. It was not meant to signify any change in their friendship or their love for her. They simply did not know that one extra invitation, one stamp, would have brought a recognition of one's continued existence. The invitation, even though it would be declined, would have said, "we're still thinking of you."

ABOUT LIVING AFTER DEATH

When we lose someone close to us, it is easy to think only of the loss. That loss will never disappear. The pain may lessen but the loss will always be there.

We can look at that life before as an exquisite picture frame that held our special memories. The memories are there but that picture frame has been shattered into hundreds of pieces. It can never be put back together as it was, but those pieces can be gathered and melded into a new and beautiful structure to hold the next picture. For those left behind that loss is the start of a new beginning.

SURVIVING

She was beautiful – dressed casually with a face that exuded calmness and kindness. "Come in and meet my husband," she said to me. Her husband lay on the bed, legs and arms thin and emaciated, reminiscent of the pictures of African children suffering from famine, weak, barely subsisting. His face was gaunt and sallow. He wore only boxer shorts for as she quickly explained, he didn't want more clothing. Perhaps the touch of any fabric, no matter how light, caused pain, or maybe just the body was closing down, needing less warmth as it withdrew from life. She touched him so gently, with such love, and spoke to him as if he were simply suffering from exhaustion or a bad case of the flu. Since I was now here, she could leave for a short while. She was going to dance class.

For a long time my patient lay quietly, appearing asleep. Then he became agitated. He rolled his body sideways, inching across the bed, so close to the edge. He seemed to want to sit up. "Would you like to sit in the chair," I asked. Incomprehensible guttural sounds were the only response. "Do you want to lay back, are you thirsty, can I get you anything?" No response, just sounds which to him maybe were enunciating his request, but to me were incomprehensible utterances. I felt frustrated with my inability to understand, that same frustration I remember when my sons were infants – the cry, the babble, their attempt to express a need, my knowledge that there was a need but no ability to understand that need, to help, to assuage the pain, the hunger, the hurt. His desperate cry accelerated my own sense of desperation at my inability to understand or to help.

My patient was young, his children were young – 12 and 17 – just teenagers dealing with their own anxieties and concerns, now having the added burden that no child should have to bear – watching their father who six months before was just their father, the one who loved them, and disciplined them, and played with them, and shared all those normal experiences we have growing up. Now their father was weak, he could not really talk, and he was leaving them. What would happen to them, what would their lives be like?

But it was to his wife that my thoughts really strayed. It brought back so many memories for me. Two sons of similar age, that need to be strong for them, to handle everything as if it were just another of life's tasks, to give them comfort and security when you yourself had none. And holding everything inside so as not to panic your children with the prospect of uncertainty and greater loss.

I wanted her to know that she would make it. She would get through the process, she would be there for her children, who because of her love and care, would not only survive, but also thrive. She would get through each day, and each day that lump in her heart would lessen.

I wanted her to know that there will be days when the sun seems to shine through you and your spirits begin to float, and then out of nowhere you catch sight of something – a young couple walking hand in hand, a father throwing a football to his son, or you overhear a conversation – a woman describing with enthusiasm the vacation she and her husband had just taken to Africa, even though you had no plans for such a trip. These sights, these tidbits of conversation come crashing down on you, sucking the sunshine from your soul and reminding you of what you have lost and will never have again.

I wanted her to know that there would be bittersweet moments, like when your child fulfills his father's dream of attending the same university, and he graduates on Father's Day and you can hardly hold back the tears so mixed with joy and sadness.

I wanted her to know that there would be new experiences and new traditions, that you and your children could now put on snowshoes and track through the forest to pick out and haul back that one special Christmas tree – a venture your husband would never agree to. You can let your children ride that go-kart he was always too fearful to allow. You have the same fear, but you will hold your breath and pray and allow them a new little space of freedom.

I wanted her to know that she would have a new life, not the one she imagined, but one that will take her in a new direction, that will provide new experiences and new adventures. She will never forget and tears will fill her eyes at the most unexpected times, but she will not only survive, she will flourish. She will dance.

THE QUESTION I STILL HAVE –

Why are we so afraid of dying?

WHY

The calls are increasing. Another friend has cancer. We are all in our late 60's or 70's. Is it the environment which has changed since our childhood? No one we knew had cancer back then. It was a word you seldom heard. Or is it that we are all getting periodic tests for everything and so discovering things sooner, when there remains a possibility of doing something? Or is it that we are living longer and generally more active and our life expectancies are greater, so our expectations are greater? But our expectations of what?

Six months before my friend had called to tell me she had been diagnosed with ovarian cancer. I calendared all of her treatment dates. This Monday would be her last chemo session. Her hair was gone, she'd gained weight, she had no energy and generally felt miserable. She was almost there – the point where you can finally start looking forward to being yourself again, where you know every day will get better. Now another threat loomed – she had the gene for breast cancer. She did not want some doctor someday to say, "You have breast cancer," so she decided to have a mastectomy.

I hung up the phone and had one strange thought -- Why? I know considerations are different if we are in our 30's, or 40's or 50's. But what about when we are in the last quarter of our lives?

We are all going to die of something. How long do you fight the odds? How long do you undergo excruciating treatment where you are no longer you? You are ugly, you are fat, you are exhausted, you can't do anything you used to do. You are not you. How long do you go through this not being you so you can be you again – for how long? Six months, two years, three years -- always living in fear, in anticipation of the next checkup. Is time – the extra day, month, year –the only significant consideration? Are those extra days – no matter how painful –always better than accepting mortality? It often seems that our fear of death surpasses everything.

The sister of one of my Hospice patients learned she had cancer. She was in her late 80's and decided to fight it. For six months she went through chemotherapy and radiation, with all its attendant miseries. At the end they told her the treatment had not been completely successful. The cancer had spread to her back and brain. She died several weeks later. I often wonder if she ever questioned her decision to fight.

Another person in his mid 70's had a prostate exam and found an elevated PSI count. He scheduled radiation. The count went down so he postponed treatment. A few months later the count rose and he started a daily three hour commute for radiation therapy. He did this for five and a half weeks. When I asked him why at his age with a slow growing cancer would he undergo the rigorous therapy, his response was he wanted to rule out prostate cancer as one of the ways he would die.

Why are we so afraid of dying?

I recently asked my Hospice patient this question and she said, "It is fear of the unknown."

I asked her, "How do you picture that unknown?"

"It is a dark void, a heavy nothingness, a complete absence of self," she responded.

"Does it have to be black and heavy," I asked. "Couldn't it be white and light?"

She thought a moment and said, "You are right. In fact many people who claim to have died and come back describe a white light."

We went back to the story I was reading. A few minutes later I looked up and saw that her eyes were closed and she appeared to be asleep. I stopped reading and held her hand. After some time she opened her eyes.

"Where were you?" I asked.

"It was white," she said, " and there was a wall. It was white too and it seemed to curve outward on both sides. I felt myself gliding forward."

"Were you afraid?" I asked.

"No," she responded immediately.

"How did you feel?" I prodded.

""Apprehensive."

"Of what?"

"I don't know," she responded. "It was just the unknown, I guess, though it was light, and it was not fear, like that fear of looking into a black deep hole."

I come back to my question – which now seems to have two parts, though maybe just flip sides of the same coin. Why are we willing to endure horrendous pain, a suspension of life as we know it, living in a body that is not the one that is ours, getting up every day not to the sunshine and possibilities but to the knowledge that you have one more day to endure, to get through, that hopefully things will improve, that you will get a respite?

I often think back on the last eight months of my husband's life – four more months than the oncologist had opined. Should we have done the first round of chemotherapy? Why did we even start the second round with a different drug, especially after the doctor told us the first drug was the one he thought had the greatest chance of success? Why did we increase the memories of a husband and father in screaming pain? Why did we turn memories of a brilliant, articulate lawyer into stark images of an incoherent mumbler? Why did we not take our two young sons out of school and go to a place where we could be together, talk, hug, hold hands, share memories and make one beautiful lasting memory of a special time together? No one discussed quality of life. Our doctor only talked about treatment.

So I come back to my question -- Is one more day so important? Will we spend our lives concentrating on just staying alive no matter the physical, financial or emotional cost?

Are we not even asking that question because we are avoiding the ultimate one – why am I afraid of dying? If my patient can change her view of the hereafter from one of darkness to one of light, or if one has a strong belief in the goodness of a god in a hereafter of bliss, can we let go of fear? Can we stop the incessant therapies and stop prolonging the agonies? Will there ever be a time when we can hug our family and friends and just say, "It's been great. Thank you all. I'm ready to go into the light."

A THOUGHT FOR THOSE LEFT

"Grief is not an event, but a passage, a pilgrimage along a path that allows us to reflect upon the past from points of remembrance held in the soul. At times the way is filled with stones under foot and we feel pained by our memories, yet on other days the shadows reflect our longing and those happinesses shared."

Jacqueline Winspear "Messenger of Truth"

ABOUT THE AUTHOR

Lesley Andrus practiced law in Los Angeles with her husband until his death. She and her two sons then moved to Sun Valley, Idaho where she became a Hospice volunteer, also serving on the Hospice Board and as its President. She has been taking care of Hospice patients for 18 years.

Made in the USA
Las Vegas, NV
24 January 2024

84857380R00073